Dear Walt & Jennie,

Hear we are again, though I'm wondering how.

You may have heard of my naval engagement with a submarine Greenery in the form of an entanglement of weeds in the River Somme on the 31st May (Wednesday). Well, I was bathing and diving in got entangled in weeds 6 feet below the surface. It was some experience for me I can assure you. I held my breath till I became unconscious and am glad to say kept my head until then – as I knew they were trying to get me. I didn't believe the man who once told me that drowning is the most pleasant death a man can die – and I certainly think he'd change his mind if he experienced it. Well I was got out after 8 minutes under water the whole time by the efforts of Pte Dominish Sharkey – who was none too good a swimmer himself and had to be rescued by Pte Potter of my Platoon before I was taken out of the water.

Sensibility began to return to me when I was seized by the head and dragged out. My nose and ears bled a little – through me holding my breath I suppose – and curiously enough I was able to get up after about two minutes and after dressing walked back to camp – since when I have carried on as usual feeling no worse for my Experience – save that I don't want the like again.

One thing did upset me and yet I felt proud that I was honoured by it, and that was when I recovered to find strong men grief stricken. It is with deep regret that I have to tell you that poor Sharkey (but for whom I might not have been here now) was killed a week later on Wednesday the 7 June while we were in the Trenches. He was fatally injured by a Rifle Grenade and died a few hours later. His heroic spirit never failed him and when the Stretcher Bearer was exercising great care in negotiating bad corners in the trench when carrying him out he said with a smile "Don't worry about being careful with me boys, I know I'm done – it's 'moving day'" He always used to recite a piece called "Moving Day" when we moved into or out of the trenches and yet this brave fellow was once discharged as "not likely to become an efficient soldier".

We even in that delightful hole (?) I told you of before – and since I came back I think ? almost been more ? in the air than out of it. There are a lot of Germans who won't trouble us any more – they didn't know who was waiting and longing for them to try their game. We know that very few regained their holes, and the Bayonets of North Countrymen who settled their claim to our Trench.

I hope you and the two ? are keeping well. I'm fairly canny excepting a cold. Had beastly cold wet weather in the trenches this time so I was glad when we quit them. Well everything in the garden's lovely (as they say) and my word there will be some fruit presently.

Well so long and let me have a line soon. Civil Soc. Note enclosed. Please keep it for me.

Love to all,
Your loving Brother,

Arthur

Same address as before after being in a part of France
recently occupied (June 30) by Germans - nearer to Berlin
7th July 1916

My dear Mother & all,

By the hand of Providence I can still say "Here we are again" – though when I think of that great charge and battle of the memorable 1st July it makes me wonder how my bulk got there and stayed there in deadly fighting with bullets & shells like rain for 36 hours continuous. I thank God I was able to keep a calm head to lead my brave men who were simply splendid and I never turned a hair all through the three days of action. Shelter Wood & Crucifix Trench were hard but we (& no one else) took it. The charge over 1200 yards of ground was the most magnificent sight I have seen & I shall never forget nor cease to marvel that human beings were capable of such calm resolution. We all were without sleep from 28-9 June to 4th July & we beat the Germans hollow. "Mercy Kamerad" they would shout after doing treacherous deeds – and we obliged them. I wish you could see my Trophies of War. The Spiked Helmet of a Prussian I downed in deadly combat & several other things.

After 3 hours in action I alone was left and led my Company to our objective & by the aid of Providence brought the noble remnants out of action after one of the most glorious displays of prowess in war that Regiment can in History place on record. The North Countrymen were too good for even the famous Prussians who whined for mercy after shooting us down with hellish Machine Gun fire to the moment we reached them. The General himself is overjoyed at our splendid work & the C-in-Chief has congratulated us too. I was lightly wounded in the knee from almost spent Shrapnel but am A1. and several bullets ripped my Tunic. My friend Lt Martin was treacherously shot through the neck by a wounded German whom he passed – but then turned and slew – the swine he deserved no mercy for treachery like that.

Shelter Wood & Crucifix Trench are all mentioned in the papers to the credit of the Royal Scots – but they were never there. They were on our left at La Boiselle. We marched from the Battlefield singing "Keep the Home Fires Burning" & every man had a German spike Helmet or other Trophy. We exterminated the 110th-111th and 186th (latter shewn in Daily Mail as 168th in error are prisoners at Southampton) Prussian Regiments.

Please tell the rest of the family as I'm too busy to write to all.
Well, dear people, I must draw to a close for the present.

With best love,

Your affectionate Son,
Arthur

8th July 1916

Dear Walt & all,

Yours received. I wasn't romancing then after all in what I said was in the air.

A week ago today, the "Glorious first of July", we attacked at 7.30am after one hours intensive bombardment coupled with mines on the left of that place. A most hellish barrage of curtain fire together with Machine Gun fire met us immediately, but though men dropped like cut corn we went through at walking pace according to orders.

It was the most wonderful and soul inspiring sight I have ever seen, and I shall never forget as long as I live the grim determined look on each face and the calm resolution displayed. The unbelievable things that happened. I was astounded when lighting my pipe as I advanced to see my men take out Cigarettes also and light up. Men dropped in hundreds wounded and dying but never a murmer did I hear – they had each determined in his heart that the Division which was slighted at Loos would prove to the world its worth – and so we pressed on until we were 50 yards from the Machine Guns firing at us – then we cut loose and charged as only North Countrymen can – and had arrived 1600 yards nearer Berlin in a very short time. We exterminated the 110th 111th and 186th Prussian Regiments (the latter referred to by Daily Mail as 168th at Southampton – Prisoners). We captured M. Guns, Field Guns, Trench Mortars etc. The glorious charge of the Royal Scots referred to in the papers when they? (stet) captured Shelter Wood & Crucifix Trench was our charge and these places & many hundred prisoners fell to us. A short time after we advanced 2nd Lt. Martin (No 12 Platoon) was shot through the neck by a wounded Hun, who got no mercy therefor. We had some hard fighting and many a brave lad went down charging Shelter Wood in face of M. Gun fire. I was in seven attempts on this place before we got it, and then we didn't forget the treacherous swine. They used reversed bullets in their rifles. Men went down all around me hit by them. It was in one of these Bayonet Charges on Shelter Wood that Lt. W. Barker of Sunderland was hit and sustained a broken thigh. In spite of the fact he refused to be moved, I picked him up and carried him to safety as they were firing on us all the time. I bandaged him and had to leave him to again lead my Company – emphasis on the my – as I was the only one left – and we took and held it – and prisoners too. We could have gone on easily but the Divisions right and left had not kept pace so we had to await them. Everything went perfectly well so far as our job was concerned – we did it and a bit more besides.

I brought the Company out of action on the evening of 4-5 July – a proud – if reduced – Company. I'm not in command though now – as a Senior Officer awaited us (coming out of action) from England. I'm glad to say I never turned a hair all through the action though I never closed my eyes from 28-29 June to evening of 5 July 1916. I thank Providence that I was able to lead my men with a clear head and shew them the way. They placed their confidence in me a long while ago. "You lead, and we'll damned well follow you anywhere" they said. They were simply splendid and went for the Huns with great dash.

My Lewis Gun Team put out over 300 Germans and we broke two Counter attacks by the famous Prussian Guards. We met them hand to hand, and bayonet to bayonet routed them. One pompous bombastic swine of a Prussian Officer glowered at me while I laid him out in good old English Style and said "You English Bastard", so I knocked him out for good. Reversed Bullets were used by them. I both captured them and saw their effects. The Prussian above mentioned wore the great Wilhelm's highest decoration. In one charge on Shelter Wood, I alone survived, but we took it soon afterwards.

The Germans can not be trusted for they are without chivalry – devilishly cunning. They whined the well known "Merci Kamerad" after "doing in" our wounded and other such like treacherous deeds.

Our Harry's Batln is carrying on the good work where we left, but he will not be with them as he is Q.M.S. I've seen one of their officers whom I know and he told me. So I may see the kid soon. Our Artillery was magnificent & our mines too.

This affair was a magnificent triumph for the Division & will suit Conan Doyle A1

Well my dear ? and all I must conclude with love to all and I am thankful to the Almighty that I have been spared from this bloody battle of which the Loos men say "Loos wasn't in it", and although I wasn't at Loos I think it couldn't be.

Love to all,

Your affectionate Brother

Arthur

Please pass to Willie as I haven't time to write to all.
Don't worry if I'm reported "killed in action" as I was given up as a gonner several times.

12th July 1916

Dear People,

Enclosed paper of mine please hand to Walter to retain. You will be glad to learn Harry & I have met again. We are quite near each other. He's in good form & his Batln has also done well.

I enclose Registered Postal Packet Receipt for package despatched addressed to Father. The trophy therein is a rare one & I want Father to take great care of it for me. I gave Hy photo of the person I got it from & he'll send them to you. All(?) are feeding well & things are splendidly organised. Harry also took a copy of something concerning me which may bear fruit.

I hope you are all keeping well. Received letter from Annie & Mirian(?) Winter(?). Her brother was wounded (near me) in the face.

Received Mothers parcel – regret not acknowledged.

Excuse more at present.

Love to all,

Your affectionate Son,

Arthur

3rd August 1916

Dear Mother & all.

Just a few lines to let you know I'm fit & well.

Please look among my Military Books & send me "Musketry Regulations", 1914 Edition (Dark Red Book about 5"x4". Also Light Blue Book on Musketry Instruction issued by the National Rifle Association, & so stated on outside cover. Also Scarlet Book "ROYAL WARRANT".

I require these (especially the latter) in my new capacity as Assistant Adjutant.

The General sent word on the 1st August that I am awarded the "Military Cross" for the scrap on 1st July – "the Glorious First"

I hope you are keeping well & all the folks. I have just left the line again & am at present on a special military course of training up to the 12th, so you will be able to send my Books here & any letter posted by the 8th will reach me here. The weather is remarkably hot. I met Gordon Baty on the 29th. He looks pretty fit.

Will you please post 3 Books at once.

I am posting my old Tunic – Hat - & also a Souvenir Hun Helmet to you in a day or so & will register them because of the latter.

Well I must close for the present. Harrys Batln is probably out resting now I think – as I've had no word since I saw him on July 19th.

Best love to all,

Your affectionate Son,
Arthur S. Morley

France as usual

10th August 1916

Dear Willy & all.

Received your letter.

No special news at present save that I am now sporting my decoration for July 1st – Military Cross.

Love to all,

Your loving Brother,
Arthur

3rd September 1916

Dear Walt & all.

Have just landed home on "Special Leave". Mary was writing you but I've got orders to do it myself.

The General drove me to the French Port in his Car, very good of him.
The Photo of Nancy and Margery is an excellent one.
All are well at home

Love to all from
Arthur & Mary

Leave 2-9.9.16

THIRTEEN DAYS LATER, LIEUTENANT ARTHUR SELWYN MORLEY WAS REPORTED MISSING HAVING BEEN KILLED IN ACTION ON SEPTEMBER 16TH 1916 DURING AN ATTACK ON GIRD TRENCH, NEAR THE TOWN OF GUEUDECOURT IN FRANCE. ARTHUR WAS 25 YEARS OLD AND HAS NO KNOWN GRAVE.

THE LIFE OF ARTHUR SELWYN MORLEY 1891 - 1916

1891

Arthur Selwyn Morley was born on June 27th 1891 at Eastgate House Farm, Weardale, in County Durham. He was the fifth son of Hannah Morley and William Morley, a hill farmer. William moved his family to Houghton-le-Spring upon his appointment as Surveyor and Health Inspector to Houghton-le-Spring Rural District Council, a post he held until his death in 1921.

1901

Arthur (10) and his family were living at 29 Edwin Street, Houghton-le-Spring.

1906

Arthur (15) and his family moved to 100 Sunderland Street, Houghton-le-Spring. Around this time he was attending the Royal Kepier Grammar School and ran with the Houghton & District Harriers.

1911

Arthur (20) was a solicitor's clerk with Legge & Miller of 1 Sunderland Street, Houghton-le-Spring.

1914

On the outbreak of war, Arthur (23) and three of his brothers joined up as Privates. Arthur's regiment was with the Durham Light Infantry and he did his training at Bullswater Camp in Woking as a Lance Corporal.

1915

Arthur (24) rapidly passed through the stages of non-commissioned rank to a commission on April 5th 1915. Arthur's promotion was listed in the London Gazette.

1916

JANUARY - Arthur (25) married Mary Crake Wilson at St Michael & All Angels Church, Houghton-le-Spring on January 13th 1916.

MAY - While off duty with the British Expeditionary Force, Arthur almost drowned when he became tangled in weed in the River Somme on May 31st 1916.

JUNE - Arthur was involved in a wire-cutting operation at Crawley Ridge Trench under very heavy fire on June 27th 1916.

JULY - Arthur advanced from the front line trenches on July 1st 1916 - the start of the Battle of the Somme - and miraculously survived the onslaught.

AUGUST - Arthur was awarded the Military Cross: "For conspicuous gallantry in action. He took command of his company when the senior officers became casualties, led several attacks on an enemy position, and behaved with great coolness and courage till the battalion was relieved."

SEPTEMBER - Arthur was at home with wife Mary on Special Leave between September 2nd - 9th 1916. He returned to the front line and was killed in action on September 16th 1916 during an attack on Gird Trench, near the town of Gueudecourt in France.
He was 25 years old.

1917

Arthur's widow, Mary, gave birth to a daughter, Muriel Selwyn Crake Wilson Morley.

1920

A marble Roll of Honour tablet was unveiled by the Earl of Durham inside St Michael & All Angels Church, Houghton-le-Spring, on December 22nd 1920. The memorial features one hundred and one names including: Lieut. A. S. MORLEY, M.C.
The design was prepared by Arthur's brother, Thomas M. Morley!

1925

A cenotaph was unveiled in the churchyard of St Michael & All Angels Church, Houghton-le-Spring, on November 7th 1925. The memorial features the names of two-hundred and thirty six individuals including: MORLEY A.S.

1932

The Thiepval Memorial, the Memorial to the Missing of the Somme, near Picardy in France was unveiled by Edward, Prince of Wales. It includes the names of more than 72,000 men who were killed in the Somme, including Arthur Selwyn Morley on Pier and Face 14A and 15C.